21-Day
Grace Challenge

Brandon Pollard, Dana Pollard

Grace Team

DEDICATION

This book is lovingly dedicated to our Lord Jesus Christ who gave his life while we were yet sinners.

This book is also dedicated to the Grace for Eternity Church Planters, who laid their life down, so we can reach others with the gospel of grace.

CONTENTS

PREFACE

Years ago, the Lord showed me a vision of Fort Worth being drenched in a tsunami. Instead of destruction and devastation to the city and the buildings, the giant wave resulted in seeing everything beautiful and clean. I believe the tsunami in my vision is the revelation of grace to the city of Fort Worth! The Lord asked us to plant a church, in our home town of more than 35 years, dedicated to the focus of the new covenant and Jesus Christ. Since the launch of Grace For Eternity Church in 2015, we have seen chains of condemnation fall away from people and their true identity in Christ manifest. Marriages have been saved, relationships restored, the sick have been healed, debt has been miraculously canceled and much, much more. We believe these blessings occurred because of the obedience of Christ Jesus and His righteousness, not our own self righteousness apart from Him.

At Grace For Eternity Church we believe Jesus is grace personified. So when you read the word "grace" feel free to see our loving savior Jesus. For out of His fullness came grace upon grace. (John 1:16)

This devotional is dedicated to the intentional focus for the next 21 days on our Lord Jesus Christ.

-Pastor Brandon Pollard

ACKNOWLEDGEMENTS

We humbly rely on the Holy Spirit for wisdom and truth. We are grateful for Spirit led leadership and pastors giving their time and gifting to support this ministry of grace. Our Grace Team Volunteers are made up of dedicated apostles, evangelists, pastors, teachers, and prophets. Because of their generosity, our church and this 21 day devotional is possible. Special thanks to those who also contributed their story in this book of their journey focusing on Jesus: Gary Seay, John and Kati Phillips, Mark and Kim Hamilton, Gail Gause. Each one of you inspire me to be a greater leader and a greater servant as Jesus came to serve. Thank you for your love and sacrifice for His bride!

-Pastor Brandon Pollard

Day 1
Grace Brings Healing

Hospital floors, in general, are very clean. At least, they appear that way when your face is laying on them. For several hours, I was face down trying to get a little bit of relief with a face that was flush. When the nurses asked what pain level I was experiencing, I told thcm a seven on a scale of one to ten.

In general, I considered myself having a high pain tolerance and figured a gunshot to the head would possibly be a ten. A knife to the throat would possibly be a nine. Birthing a baby would possibly be an eight, and this pain I was experiencing had to be a seven! I understand now that many who have gone through any of the above may disagree; but to me, it made sense at the time. The problem was I didn't know that describing a pain level of only seven doesn't get you seen by doctors right away!

This was a glimpse of a three-year window when I averaged only three hours of sleep each night. Many times, I would wake up with a fever in the middle of the night, and my whole body would ache.

On this day, I actually knew what was happening to my body; I was experiencing a kidney stone! The nurses sent me to the waiting room and I couldn't sit down in a chair because the pain was so intense. Like an infant in the fetal position, there I lay in the hospital bathroom with my face to the cold tile floor, next to the toilet, and I prayed a great prayer of faith. It went like this, "GOD, EITHER KILL ME OR HEAL ME!"

It would be great to tell you that from the amazing prayer of faith, and from that moment on, I never felt pain again, but that just wasn't the case. Even though I no longer had kidney stones, pain and fever persisted. The doctors ordered many tests, but couldn't find what was wrong. Even after attending healing meetings, prayer lines, and "life-changing" retreats, I still wasn't healed.

Then one day, I was praying and the Lord revealed to me that I was trying to earn God's healing instead of resting in the favor of Jesus. He showed me that I was searching to see if my behavior was worthy to receive healing, and if I was good enough, then I thought I would be healed. Now instead of searching my behavior, I search for the favor that I already have in Jesus. As I meditated on Jesus and that He is the only way to gain favor, in less than 21 days, Jesus completely healed my body!
— Brandon Pollard

Scripture Meditation:

Psalm 103:2-5 (English Standard Version)

Bless the Lord, O my soul,   and forget not all his benefits,   who forgives all your iniquity,   who heals all your diseases,   who redeems your life from the pit,   who crowns you with steadfast love and mercy,   who satisfies you with good   so that your youth is renewed like the eagle's.

Grace Challenge:

Ask the Lord if you have believed you don't deserve His favor based on your behavior. Meditate and rest on the complete obedience of Jesus and His good works. Thank Him that because of His obedience, you are granted, by grace, the favor of God! Write down the spontaneous thoughts that flow as you seek the Lord:

_____

_____

_____

_____

_____

_____

_____

_____

_____

_____

_____

_____

_____

_____

_____

_____

Day 2
No Room For Condemnation

A few years ago, I was boarding a plane from Georgia to go home to Texas and really didn't want to be bothered with small talk. I was tired from a long work conference and was ready to get home to my family. The first hour of the flight, I didn't say anything to the stranger beside me, probably hoping he wouldn't say anything back. That's right; I wasn't prayed up, or super spiritual. I was tired and all I could think about was how much I missed my smoking hot wife.

When the man beside me started a conversation about the Christian book I was reading, I couldn't help but make eye contact out of politeness. He began to tell me how he volunteered for years in the church, never missing a Sunday. He went on to tell me about all the great spiritual things he had done for the Lord in his church. For some reason, words came out of my mouth that I have never said, and I'm not so sure I will say ever again. I stated this, "Do you know why so many Christians commit suicide?"

Who says this?! Who says this to a perfect stranger, let alone to a close intimate friend? Alarms and danger warnings were sounding off in my head even while the words were coming out of my mouth. I began to tell him that many Christians think God is judging them for every sin. I opined that even though Jesus came to the earth to save the world and not judge it, they believe God is still judging Christians for every sin. Then I began to explain briefly about Romans 8:1, that it saved my life and saved my marriage.

The man began to sob uncontrollably. He began to tell me that his brother committed suicide and his sister overdosed on drugs, which he believed was an act of suicide. Worse, he believed his son was now struggling with thoughts of suicide. This man had been judging others his whole life, the way he thought God was judging him.

Before we prayed together on that plane, I told him this was no accident we met each other and the Lord wanted to tell Him that there is now NO CONDEMNATION from God for those who are in Christ Jesus! He didn't have to feel condemned for the death of his family or for his sin. Christ became sin so that we would become the righteousness of God in Christ Jesus. (2 Corinthians 5:21)
— Brandon Pollard

Scripture Meditation:
Romans 8:1 (English Standard Version)
Therefore, there is now no condemnation (judgment) for those who are in Christ Jesus.

Grace Challenge:

Ask the Father today if you have believed a lie that He is judging you in an area of weakness.

Ask Him for the truth about that area of weakness and how He truly sees you. Thank Him for passing no condemnation on you!

Ask the Lord if there is anyone in your family or friends that need to know there is no condemnation in Christ Jesus. Pray for them and ask if He would have you reach out to them.

_____

_____

_____

_____

_____

_____

_____

_____

_____

_____

_____

_____

_____

_____

_____

_____

Day 3
Grace Empowers Love

Before I understood the power of grace, I tried really hard to change my husband. And I didn't understand why he couldn't just get his act right! I was constantly looking to him to make me feel loved, but found only hurt instead. We constantly struggled against each other and judged every detail of each other's faults.

One day, the Lord gently whispered to me, "Without Christ, your sin is just as bad as the worst sinner on the planet, and I still loved you and laid my life down for you." I realized the wretchedness of my own sin. And the more I meditated on His forgiveness, the more I could love my husband, even before his behavior changed. If Christ could love me, I could love others!

When we discover the grace He extends to us, it gives us the power to love others even when their behavior hurts.

— Dana Pollard

Scripture Meditation:
Romans 5:8 (New International Version)
But God demonstrates his own love for us in this: While we were still sinners, Christ died for us.

Grace Challenge:

Meditate on how Christ forgave you at your worst, and listen for Him to tell you how much he loves you in your prayer time. Visualize yourself (in your holy imagination) talking with Jesus and ask him what his thoughts are toward you. Then when empowered with His love, go tell someone you love, "I forgive you and love you no matter what!"

Day 4
Breathe Grace

Last summer, I was on my way to Belize for my first father-son mission trip. With a short flight ahead of me, the flight attendants went through the instructions and procedures in case of an emergency. As I looked around at the passengers, I couldn't help but notice some people sleeping throughout the presentation. Other people were talking to one another, and some were oblivious, listening to their headphones.

My imagination couldn't help but visualize the following scene: As the flight is halfway over and passengers are sitting comfortably in their chairs, suddenly turbulence violently shakes the plane! The lights go off. Oxygen in the cabin has stopped working and the cabin pressure is low. The pit of everyone's stomach begins to shoot towards their heart as the plane starts plummeting. The oxygen masks drop promptly from above their heads.

Did they listen to the instructions? Do they put them on? One person is desperately offering to help put the masks on others, without regard for themselves. Did they listen to the instructions? They clearly said to put your mask on before attending to others. One mother panics and tries to grab her child and put the mask on the child before even thinking about putting her own on. It doesn't work, without oxygen to their brain, now they are both passed out. Screams are echoing all over the plane, as they cannot wake the sleeping people. Why wouldn't people be able to do something so simple?

These are horrific thoughts, made up from the imagination of my brain. Pictures are painted in my head from flight attendants all around the country. They calmly instruct us at the beginning of the flight, in case of an emergency, to place the air mask on ourselves first before helping others.

We all know that Jesus is life and according to John, out of His fullness is grace upon grace. Did you know that when we meditate on Jesus, we are breathing grace? Paul declared we need an abundance of grace to reign in life. So saying you have enough grace, that you don't need to spend more time meditating on Jesus, is like saying you had plenty of oxygen before you got on the plane, so you should be good. The pilot is God and yes, you will arrive at your destination (Heaven) but beloved, you'd better learn how to breathe grace! Otherwise, you will be disoriented and pass out when life gives you turbulence (trials) and low cabin pressure (tribulation)!

— Brandon Pollard

Scripture Meditation:

2 Peter 3:18 (English Standard Version)

But grow in the grace and knowledge of our Lord and Savior Jesus Christ. To him be the glory both now and to the day of eternity. Amen.

Grace Challenge:

Ask Him to reveal His love for you in whatever trial you are in right now. Meditate on how he proved his love by laying his life down for yours and saved you by his abundant grace. Find someone today who is in a trial and needs to breathe grace and offer them Jesus.

Day 5
Grace is Enough

You may have heard the Bible comparing us to sheep. Sheep are not known for being the most intelligent members of the animal kingdom. God is not comparing us to sheep to insult us. God is comparing us to sheep to instruct us. He wants us to learn more about how good our Shepherd is. God calls us sheep because sheep don't need backpacks or saddles. They are not burden-bearing animals. We weren't designed to carry our burdens. We were designed to follow our Shepherd.

In Psalm 23, the psalmist is describing our relationship with our Shepherd. It describes how He takes care of, protects and guides us. How right in the middle of the battle, He extends an invitation: not to take up arms, but to pull up a chair. Inviting us to come sit at a feast that He has prepared, and enjoy Him so much that our cup overflows. At His table, there is no lack. His grace is enough.

Because grace is enough, we don't have to add to it. We are not trying to earn God's favor, or hope that if we serve in the church or give, He will love us more. We can serve, love, and give simply because we love Jesus, the church and people. We know we will always have enough. We can fully receive this grace and aggressively give it away, because His grace is enough.

— Gary Seay

Scripture Meditation:

2 Corinthians 12:9 (English Standard Version)

But he said to me, "My grace is sufficient for you, for my power is made perfect in weakness." Therefore I will boast all the more gladly of my weaknesses, so that the power of Christ may rest upon me.

Grace Challenge:

Ask Jesus today to give you a fresh revelation of the sufficiency of His grace. Ask Him to help you rest in the knowledge that He will take care of you.

_____

_____

_____

_____

_____

_____

_____

_____

_____

_____

_____

_____

_____

_____

_____

Day 6
Grace Changes What You See

Have you ever seen a FedEx truck? Of course, you have. Did you know that they have an arrow in their logo? Right there between the "E" and the "X". For years, I never actually noticed it. One day, someone pointed out to me. Now it seems obvious. Now I can't "un-see" it.

That's the way grace is. It changes how we see things. Once our eyes are opened to the truth of His grace, and how that grace applies to every area of our lives, it changes the way we see. We see ourselves differently. We see others differently. We see our circumstances differently. We just don't see the same. The Bible says, "Taste and see that the Lord is good!" Did you know some people can taste the same goodness from God but see something different?

Some people see God as angry or judging them for every failure, but our perception is our reception. If we perceive God trying to punish us for our poor behavior, then we will receive trials in life as Him punishing us for our poor behavior. Jesus bore the judgment of our sins on the cross and He didn't come to judge you but to save you! (John 12:47). The good news is the Father and the Son are one. Jesus Christ is the same yesterday, today and forever but your thoughts of Him towards you can change often.
— Gary Seay

Scripture Meditation:

Psalm 34:8 (English Standard Version)

Oh, taste and see that the Lord is good! Blessed is the man who takes refuge in him!

Grace Challenge:

Ask the Lord what He sees. When Jesus looks at you, at your spouse, your job, your health, the church, what does He see? Ask Him to show you His perspective, and by grace help you to see through His eyes.

_____

_____

_____

_____

_____

_____

_____

_____

_____

_____

_____

_____

_____

_____

_____

_____

_____

Day 7
Grace Removes Fear

Another great night of camping with the family and I can't remember if something woke me or I hadn't quite fallen asleep but I noticed something moving not six feet from my head! There was a couch in the camper right next to our bed and on the arm of the couch was a large squirrel. My eyes were adjusting to the light in the camper and I could see it standing on its hind legs.

Wait…this was no squirrel…my eyes were adjusting even more. This was a huge disgusting rat! Gross! I immediately began to think of how I could kill it without waking the kids. If I threw my shoes at it, it would only scare it. The thought actually came to me that this rat might try on my shoes and chase me if I miss! This thing was huge! R.O.U.S. (Princess Bride Movie reference) a rodent of unusual size.

I did what any rough and tough man camping would do, I turned to my wife and nudged her awake. I said "Dana (in a whisper, slight panic), there is a rat in the camper!" Her response didn't bring any comfort to my distress, she murmured a whisper after being awoken, saying, "That rat has probably been here the whole time, just leave it alone, go back to sleep!" Well, that answer wasn't good enough for me because my eyes are now wide as saucers while I watch the rat scamper around the floor of the camper. So I nudge her again this time a little more emphatically. "Dana, Dana (still trying to whisper as to not wake up the kids), will you switch spots with me?"

Fear is not something we are born with. It is something we are taught. So who is teaching us fear? Is it God? You might be thinking to yourself, "Didn't He tell us to fear Him?" The Greek word for fear is *phobos* which means terror, alarm and also reverence and respect. We learn from scripture that we are not to have fear in the world (terror, alarm) but godly fear (reverence and respect).

Just think, did Jesus have terror, alarm about the world around Him? The answer is no. Did Jesus have terror or alarm about God? The answer is a resounding no, because He had faith in a loving Father. I want to remind you today, that you are loved by the Father just as much as He loves Jesus!
— Brandon Pollard

Scripture Meditation:
2 Timothy 1:7 (English Standard Version)
For God gave us a spirit not of fear but of power and love and self-control.

Grace Challenge:

Ask the Lord about the most fearful moment in your life. Where was He when you feared? What was His heart toward you in that moment? Ask the Lord to show you love instead of fear.

_____

_____

_____

_____

_____

_____

_____

_____

_____

_____

_____

_____

_____

_____

_____

_____

_____

Day 8
Grace Brings Hope

Sometimes, it's easy to read the stories of the Bible and forget that these events happened to real people. We have the benefit of history to know how God came through. But, in that moment, they didn't know yet what God was going to do.

The children of Israel didn't know what was going to happen at the Red Sea. All they knew was they had a body of water they couldn't cross on one side and an enemy they couldn't defeat on the other. Then God moved. The story changed. Hope replaced their fear.

Today, the Lord wants us to understand that He is still changing stories. Your story is not over. Your situation may look hopeless, but grace brings hope. We can have hope no matter how scary it looks, because God is able, and God is good.

— Gary Seay

Scripture Meditation:

Romans 15:13 (English Standard Version)

May the God of hope fill you with all joy and peace in believing, so that by the power of the Holy Spirit you may abound in hope.

Grace Challenge:

Ask the Lord to infuse you with fresh hope. Rest your heart in the knowledge that God is good, He is able, and He will come through for you.

_____

_____

_____

_____

_____

_____

_____

_____

_____

_____

_____

_____

_____

_____

_____

_____

Day 9
Grace Brings Truth

There was a time when I believed I had to find a way to stop whatever sin I was committing at the time, spend more time reading the Bible and praying, in order for God to love me more. I thought it was the only way He would not be disappointed with me.

The truth is, God loves me so much, He sent Jesus into this world as a sacrifice (or gift) for my salvation. The funny thing is, if I had understood God's grace, I probably would have opened the Bible and talked with God more. Then with the focus off myself (and that sin), I probably would have stopped whatever sin I was involved with quicker!

If you were saved by grace, then learn to live every day in God's grace. He is not mad at you. He is not punishing you or allowing you to be sick, poor, and disgusted. He is not ignoring you and leaving you to figure things out. God already made you righteous through Jesus (Romans 5:17). When the Heavenly Father looks at you, He sees Jesus (1 John 4:7). Your responsibility is to receive all that God has made available to you through Jesus. We receive salvation by putting faith in God's grace. Once we have it, we do not have to bargain for God's favor and blessing.

— Mark Hamilton

Scripture Meditation:

Colossians 2:6-7 (New King James Version)

As you therefore have received Christ Jesus the Lord, so walk in Him, rooted and built up in Him and established in the faith, as you have been taught, abounding in it with thanksgiving.

Grace Challenge:

Look in the mirror and tell yourself that you are righteous. As you walk your day out today, declare out loud, "I am righteous!" There is no other voice that you trust more than your own. Start to line your voice up with God's Word and you will begin to see yourself the way God sees you.

_____

_____

_____

_____

_____

_____

_____

_____

_____

_____

_____

_____

_____

_____

_____

_____

_____

Day 10
Grace Invests Seeds

My husband, Mark, and I have been praying for some things for several years that the Word of God says are ours as His children. We have not, yet, seen our harvest. Though we could easily get discouraged, we are confident in the Word of God. We have sown the seeds in our heart. They have taken root and are continuing to grow in us. We have chosen to believe His promises are true.

"For ALL the promises of God in Him are Yes, and in Him Amen, to the glory of God THROUGH US (2 Corinthians 1:20 New King James Version, emphasis added). Promises are seeds because they are the Word of God (2 Peter 1:2-4). The provision is all there, but it's what we do with it that makes all the difference. Just because you believe in corn doesn't mean you will harvest some corn. You have to actually SOW corn. You have to plant the seed and tend to it. Only then will you see a harvest.

God gave us the seed of His Word. Not one promise shall fail! Find them and sow them deep into your heart. Meditate on them day and night. Allow them to take root and grow in you. This will help you go beyond emotional faith to true faith. It's not about what you feel, but what has been planted in your heart and allowed to come to full fruit. That is the foundation to reaping from the promises of God.

The Bible is all about increase. It's built into the Kingdom. Within every seed lies a harvest and within every harvest is more seed. Every part of us that has the life of God in it should be increasing. "I have come that they might have life and have it more abundantly" ... INCREASE. "Seek ye first the Kingdom of God and all these things shall be added unto you." ... INCREASE.

— Kim Hamilton

Scripture Meditation:

Psalm 115:14 (King James Version)

The Lord shall increase you more and more, you and your children.

Grace Challenge:

Take the time today to sow the Word of God in your heart. Need healing? Meditate on His healing promises and believe. Need provision or peace? Meditate on the promises and believe.

Day 11
Grace Heals Families

It was a long, rocky, dusty road before receiving the revelation of God's grace. My attention was usually on what was "right" and what was "wrong" (the tree of the knowledge of good and evil) with myself and others. When I received the revelation of grace, I began to receive the reality of who God says I am and to partake of the "tree of life" for myself.

The revelation of grace has and still is completely changing my life and the relationships around me. You would think that the easiest people to extend grace to would be the loved ones that you live with everyday...right? Well, I found out very quickly, that is not the case. I expected more from them than I did from other people. We want to portray this perfect, loving Christian family... right?

Whenever Randy, my husband, would get angry or the kids would disobey, I would be mortified and usually, a tongue lashing would commence. My perfect family image was cracking and breaking piece by piece... Until one day, the Holy Spirit showed me that life and death are in the power of the tongue (Proverbs 18:21). A woman builds her home, (by her words) but a foolish woman tears it down (by her words) (Proverbs 14:1). This truth changed my perspective, and my conversations, by reminding me my family was covered by His grace and mercy.

My eyesight changed. I began to see them as God sees them and to speak grace-filled words of life over them. We are all on a journey learning how to apply the grace of God for ourselves and others.

— Gail Gause

Scripture Meditation:

Colossians 4:6 (New International Version)

Let our conversations be always filled with grace, seasoned with salt, so that you may know how to answer everyone.

Grace Challenge:

Confess out loud over those in your home that they are the righteousness of God in Christ Jesus. Confess out loud that they are holy because Christ is holy. Thank the Lord that they are forgiven 100% as you are forgiven in Christ. Ask the Lord to help them see that about themselves.

Day 12
Grace Invests In People

While visiting friends in the state of Washington, my wife and I found ourselves going white water rafting up near Mount Rainier. At the beginning of the trip, the guide reminded us of the dangers and told us what to do if we fall in the ice cold water. The group of friends we went with were full of experienced rafters and encouraged us, as they knew we were really nervous. The raft in front of us was full of college kids with a guide. It was a little more comforting to see another raft hit the rough waters each time before we did. After thirty minutes of rough water then calm, our arms were tiring. The guide told us to get ready for the roughest part of the river. We watched as the raft in front of us disappeared over the drop off and we braced to do the same.

As we hit the tremendous incline, the huge rocks were everywhere causing the water to rush over the raft, hitting my face and limiting my sight. My whole body was being sprayed constantly with water and I had to wipe my eyes to see where exactly we were rowing. I saw in front of us a raft completely tipped over with no one in it! We were in a really long stretch of rough water and now these kids were screaming for help in the freezing water. I could see one guy pinned against a huge rock by the sheer force of the water. His face was safely above water but he was holding his broken fingers in the air and it was too late to rescue him as he was just out of reach, we were forced to keep rowing. Another kid was floating on his back with his life vest and his feet forward. The guide beside me leaned over our raft and pulled him in with one hand while continuing to bark orders for us to row. You see, he was in the back directing us with his voice and using his paddle as a rudder around the rocks. It seemed like forever but we finally made it to calm water. The great news is those kids made it out alive that day but were extremely cold and had a few broken bones.

I discovered that river rafting is way more fun and safe if you stay in the boat with others. Jesus promised to never leave us nor forsake us, but we can certainly put ourselves in danger that He didn't intend for us to be in. I have tried in the past to do things on my own, such as taking risks He didn't approve. I found I desperately needed him to rescue me from my decisions, my circumstances, to pull me out of the water into a safe place where others care.
— Brandon Pollard

Scripture Meditation:
Psalm 91:14-16 (English Standard Version)
Because he holds fast to me in love, I will deliver him;
I will protect him, because he knows my name.
When he calls to me, I will answer him;
I will be with him in trouble;
I will rescue him and honor him.
With long life I will satisfy him and show him my salvation

Grace Challenge:

Have you ever felt like you were drowning in chaos and pain? Do you remember the Lord rescuing you? Ask the Lord to show you someone who is drowning in pain. Invite them to coffee, let them know you are praying for them. Encourage them to surround themselves with other believers.

_____

_____

_____

_____

_____

_____

_____

_____

_____

_____

_____

_____

_____

_____

_____

_____

Day 13
Grace Gives Eternal Security

A good friend of mine had three biological sons and adopted five more children in a short amount of time. Preparing for a lesson on adoption that weekend, I invited him in into my office to talk face to face. Who would have a better grasp of the Father's love for adoption than someone who was living it?

After a passionate and deep conversation, I discovered that each child was different in personalities but secretly had one thing in common, hidden among their thoughts. You see, each adopted child had to overcome thoughts of being "returned".

The adopted parents had a role to play in this and so did the siblings. I was in tears listening to the thought of a child wondering if their behavior was going to make them disowned. Some of his children didn't trust him right away. So after being adopted, they had a "show me" kind of attitude exhibiting bad behavior, secretly and tremendously hoping that they could "keep" these parents.

There is a deadly doctrine spreading around the church today in Fort Worth and other parts of the world called "Lordship Salvation." The title sounds wonderful, even Biblical. The mega pastors have said from the pulpit, "If He's not Lord of every area of your life, He's not Lord of any area of your life!" They will say, "There are people in this room who think they are saved, but are going to hell because He will say 'I never knew you.'" quoting Jesus from Matthew 7:21.

These pastors have good intentions. Their heart is that people would surrender more of their behavior to Jesus and do good works. The altars flood with Christians, because they don't know if they are truly saved. But Jesus goes on to say in verse 22, their behavior *was* surrendered to the many good works, as evident in their argument: "Did we not prophesy in your name, cast out demons in your name, do many mighty works in your name?"

Salvation can't be earned. You can't do more to try to become a part of the family or to not be returned. Salvation is by faith alone in Jesus, not by works.

But what happens if your faith stumbles on your worst day? Does He return you? Did God's adoption of you really work or is it temporary, based on your performance of surrendering? I'm curious, do we think we did something to deserve to be adopted?

Jesus said, "And this is the will of God, that I should not lose even one of all those he has given me, but that I should raise them up at the last day" (John 6:39).
— Brandon Pollard

Scripture Meditation:

Ephesians 2:4-9 (English Standard Version)

But God, being rich in mercy, because of the great love with which he loved us, even when we were dead in our trespasses, made us alive together with Christ—by grace you have been saved—and raised us up with him and seated us with him in the heavenly places in Christ Jesus, so that in the coming ages he might show the immeasurable riches of his grace in kindness toward us in Christ Jesus. For by grace you have been saved through faith. And this is not your own doing; it is the gift of God, not a result of works, so that no one may boast.

Grace Challenge:

Settle in your heart today that you are saved through faith in Jesus alone, for eternity. Thank Him that the Holy Spirit is inside of you, and has sealed you (Ephesians 1:13). Thank Him that He will never leave or forsake you (Hebrews 13:5). Remind yourself of the day you were baptized by water, when you were buried in Christ and a new creation. If you have never been baptized, talk with a pastor to get baptized.

_____

_____

_____

_____

_____

_____

_____

_____

_____

_____

_____

_____

_____

_____

_____

_____

_____

_____

Day 14
Grace is the Source of Life

It was a spring day, I had just graduated Bible school, had a beautiful new bride, and our first child was on the way. I should have been on top of the world, but inside I was clinging onto the last shred of hope I had to be free. What nobody knew, except my wife, was that I had been struggling with a sexual addiction for over 10 ten years. Today, I was hoping to finally be free. I had heard countless sermons on discipleship and how, by God's grace, we can be free if we just believed. The messages were all the same; your belief was defined by your lifestyle. If you believed, you would do anything and give up anything for God.

I believed and had tried hard to force my way to God by doing everything I knew how. All I wanted was to be free of the demons that controlled me. This would be my deliverance day! I had proven my commitment; studied for two years, sold all I had, and destroyed all my vices. Yet my mind still focused on what my flesh wanted. Today, I was going to finally be rid of my curse!

Mustering all my courage up, I went to see the deliverance pastor. Full of guilt, shame, and humility, I confessed all my sins in great detail. Then he prayed and I walked out feeling violated as I heard him say the same works-based rhetoric that had failed me for years, "Now that you're free, go out, pray, read your Bible, press into God, and truly believe you're a new creation."

What does that even mean? I was done, completely defeated at my attempts to get to God through my actions. I didn't understand anything about grace, and in fact, the word grace just reminded me of my failure. This day, I started to experience the person of grace instead of the thought of grace. It was at the lowest point of my life, in my deepest despair, with no more options left to "work" my way into God's presence, that God came to me. Gently, grace began to talk to me, and I eventually came out of my despair not only free of bondage but into a deep connection with the one who is truth.

When Jesus died, He restored our connection to God the Father, which was something that Adam and Eve had broken. This is redemption; restoration back to the status we had before sin (before the fall of man) and back to the 'time' prior to sin's existence in our life! Grace gives us the ability to hit the reset button and start over!
— John Phillips

Scripture Meditation:
John 14:6 (English Standard Version)
Jesus said to him, "I am the way, and the truth, and the life. No one comes to the Father except through me."

Grace Challenge:

Imagine you are walking in the garden in the cool evening with the Father, exchanging breath in conversation. Breathe out your failure, allow Him to speak and breathe in His grace.

Write down His answer:

_____

_____

— _____

_____

_____

_____

_____

_____

_____

_____

_____

_____

_____

_____

_____

_____

_____

_____

_____

Day 15
Grace Brings Double Honor

For three months or more, the Lord impressed on me to stay and meditate on Isaiah 61. Over and over, I would read it aloud, adding my name to personalize it. As I was studying Isaiah, the Lord reminded me when I was eight years old, I once stood on the side of a stage that overlooked ten thousand people on a soccer field. The evangelist, my parents had invited, was preaching in Papua New Guinea where we were missionaries. As I watched from the side witnessing countless miracles, the Lord spoke to my heart; I was called to pastor.

From that point on, the enemy heaped shame and doubt on me, for each of the many sins and mistakes I collected over the years. One thing I was most ashamed of was when I was twenty-one, only a week away from completing Bible School, but failed. I remember being called into the office with one week left before graduation. The leaders explained to me that I had been more than 10 minutes late (twice) throughout the past year and that I had recently turned in five pages of homework with one-page blank. They told me I had three strikes against me and would have to repeat the entire year over.

Watching as my wife and friends went up on stage without me to get their diplomas, all I could do was fake a smile the entire day. Something died on the inside of me that day; the calling of God on my life was buried in shame.

Fast forward over thirteen years later (to my time in Isaiah), I sat down for lunch with a lead pastor of a large church in Fort Worth who invited me to come on staff full time as a family pastor. Although I was excited about what the Lord was doing, there was doubt in the back of my mind full of shame.

That same week, I got a message from the former dean of the Bible school, who I hadn't talked with in more than a decade, to meet for coffee. After catching up, he explained to us they were planting a church that year. He and his wife invited us and said they would love for us to come and be on staff as pastors. Of course, we had to respectively decline because we just had committed to Fort Worth, but as we were leaving in the car, I was confused and asked the Lord what that was all about. This is what the Lord whispered to my spirit, "Son, I promised I would bring you *double honor for shame*."
— Brandon Pollard

Scripture Meditation:
Isaiah 61:7 (New Living Translation)
Instead of shame and dishonor,   you will enjoy a double
share of honor.   You will possess a double portion of
prosperity in your land,   and everlasting joy will be yours.

Grace Challenge:

Ask the Lord, "Where have I received shame the most?" Did it come from the Lord? What is His heart towards your shame? Will you trust Him with it?

_____

_____

_____

_____

_____

_____

_____

_____

_____

_____

_____

_____

_____

_____

_____

_____

_____

Day 16
Grace Filters the Law

As a missionary kid, I remember when pouring a glass of water, there were tiny worms left in the strainer. Pouring our kitchen faucet water through an actual metal strainer was a daily routine.

Later when we returned to the United States, I had a friend who had a great big pool and we loved to play in it all the time. In Fort Worth, it gets extremely hot in the summer so we would jump in the pool and spend hours of fun just coming up with games and laughing. I remember one year, when summer was getting close, the pool was extremely green with moss. Concerned, I asked my friend what could be done to fix this. Turned out the pump that helped filter the water was broken. Once a beautiful pool, it was no longer used or enjoyed, and for the entire summer, that pump stayed broken!

Paul said there are two types of ministries in the Bible. The first one was the ministry of condemnation; also known as the ministry of death, or the law. The second was the ministry of righteousness; also known as the ministry of life. We describe this as the finished work of Jesus. (Found in 2 Corinthians 3)

The Lord showed me to meditate on the ministry of

righteousness and New Covenant teaching. I realized I was not taught to distinguish Bible between the two, nor was I shown how to filter everything through the New Covenant. When I read my Bible, mixed up between the two ministries, Christ became no effect, as Paul warned in Galatians.

The old covenant said I needed a clean heart. The new covenant said He had to crucify and bury my old man and heart (it was too dirty to clean). God gave me a new heart and hid me in Christ Jesus. The old covenant says, 'Take not your Holy Spirit from me,' while the new covenant says, 'I have sealed you with the Holy Spirit and will never leave.' The old covenant says, 'Have big faith and obey, and then you will be righteous.' The new covenant says, 'Jesus will start and finish your faith and give you the free gift of righteousness.' The old covenant says, 'Remember every sin, repent and you will be forgiven,' but the new covenant says, 'I will remember your sins no more, you were forgiven at the cross.'

After the Lord showed me to filter the covenants, I could see the new covenant was the good news! Why would I want to go back to the old ministry of death? If we choose to mix the two ministries, our lives will end up quite muddy!
— Brandon Pollard

Scripture Meditation:

Ephesians 2:13-15 (English Standard Version)

But now in Christ Jesus you who once were far off have been brought near by the blood of Christ. For he himself is our peace, who has made us both one and has broken down in his flesh the dividing wall of hostility by abolishing the law of commandments expressed in ordinances, that he might create in himself one new man in place of the two, so making peace.

Grace Challenge:

Ask the Lord to open your eyes to filter God's Word through grace. Are there scriptures that scare you or confuse you? Ask the Holy Spirit to reveal grace and the New Covenant.

_____

_____

_____

_____

_____

_____

_____

_____

_____

_____

_____

_____

_____

_____

_____

_____

_____

Day 17
Grace Loves the Church

Have you ever met a Christian who has made a decision to no longer attend church? Many believers have been really hurt by people in the local church, and have allowed bitterness to rise up in their hearts against the church. I'm concerned they don't understand the "why" behind church and have been deceived by the enemy to believe a lie. Grace loves the church, let me show you why.

Jesus told Peter how He was going to build His church (Matthew 16:18) on the foundation of Himself and the church would be victorious against the gates of hell. Jesus added 3,000 believers to His church in one day! The following is what scripture says:

And they devoted themselves to the apostles' teaching and the fellowship, to the breaking of bread and the prayers... and day by day, attending the temple together and breaking bread in their homes, they received their food with glad and generous hearts, praising God and having favor with all the people. And the Lord added to their number day by day those who were being saved (Acts 2:42-46 English Standard Version)

The "why" for the body of Christ gathering together was for teaching, fellowship, breaking of bread, and prayers. Much of the church leadership and operation used today in church is taken directly from God's Word. Separating ourselves from the practical gathering of believers means we have chosen to disqualify the way Jesus wants to bless our life through the church. The size of the gathering is irrelevant to God but Jesus is glorified when two or more gather in His name.

Many Christians have abandoned the local church not understanding God's heart. Yes, we are the church (the body of Christ), and we attend the four walls of a church simply to encourage and love each other. Please consider finding a church to attend if you are not currently doing so. Be a blessing to the body, and choose to serve in love, forgiving one another, regardless of other's behaviors.

— Brandon Pollard

Scripture Meditation:
Hebrews 10:24-25 (English Standard Version)
And let us consider how to stir up one another to love and good works, not neglecting to meet together, as is the habit of some, but encouraging one another, and all the more as you see the Day drawing near.

Grace Challenge:

Ask the Lord His thoughts about the local church. Has church leadership ever disappointed you? Do they need the same forgiveness you have received? Does Jesus still love the local church when they fail?

_____

_____

_____

_____

_____

_____

_____

_____

_____

_____

_____

_____

_____

_____

_____

_____

_____

_____

_____

Day 18
Grace Empowers Generosity

Did you know there is a "knee-jerk reaction" that happens when we talk about the generosity of God? The medical word for where the term "knee jerk" originated is called mono-synaptic response. The hit to the knee causes the thigh muscle to stretch. This stretch sends a signal to the spinal cord and then to the thigh muscle. So it never gets to the brain. It is not a thought-out decision to react to the mallet, however is poses a serious problem if there is no reaction.

We all have a positive or negative reaction when we hear of God's generosity. This reaction is in the backbone of our perception of God, quite possibly clouded by our circumstances and our opinions. It takes faith to go through trials and tribulations and still believe God is generous!

We are learning to walk by faith in God as a disciple of Jesus. The very backbone/foundation of our belief hinges on the questions, "Is God generous? Is He good and gracious?" Our knee-jerk reaction to His generosity and grace to others will immediately tell us about our backbone and perception of Him. It is really difficult to be generous to others when you believe God is not generous. Be encouraged fellow believer, that he who began a good work in you will bring it to completion!

— Brandon Pollard

Scripture Meditation:

Philippians 4:19 (English Standard Version)

And my God will supply every need of yours according to His riches in glory in Christ Jesus.

Grace Challenge:

If you go out to eat at a restaurant today, match the tip to the amount of the bill. Tell them face to face the Lord loves them and is generous towards them. Ask them if they need prayer and pray right there together.

_____

_____

_____

_____

_____

_____

_____

_____

_____

_____

_____

_____

_____

_____

_____

_____

_____

_____

_____

Day 19
Grace is the Pure Gospel

Back in the 90's, baseball home run records were seemingly being broken weekly. Only we found out, most of our favorite athletes in that era were taking some kind of illegal substance (performance-enhancing drugs). The side effects were destructive to the players and the game of baseball.

It's amazing how sports can mirror the everyday Christian life. There is an illegal substance in the Kingdom of God. Paul addressed it in Galatians 3, but today, let's modernize it a little, and call it the performance-enhancing gospel (P.E.G.).

Illegal Drug P.E.G. – The lie that God's love and His favor can be earned by our performance (which every religion in the world believes about their god, except Christianity).
Side effects: bipolar Christianity which asks and wonders, "He loves me…He loves me not" — the performance roller coaster with highs of self-righteousness and lows of unworthiness based on performance.

Remember the first time you heard the pure gospel? You believed that God loved you, right there in your moment of life, while you were still a sinner. God sent His Son Jesus to die and become sin for you, so that you could have a right relationship with God. You were excited because not once in your whole life was your performance good enough for God. You accepted Jesus as your Lord, he forgave your sins, saved you, and you felt highly favored and loved! Don't accept anything but the pure gospel (faith in Jesus) and reject every illegal substance offered by religion (faith in works).

— Brandon Pollard

Scripture Meditation:

Galatians 3:1-3 (English Standard Version)

O foolish Galatians! Who has bewitched you? It was before your eyes that Jesus Christ was publicly portrayed as crucified. Let me ask you only this: Did you receive the Spirit by works of the law or by hearing with faith? Are you so foolish? Having begun by the Spirit, are you now being perfected by the flesh?

Grace Challenge:

Ask the Lord for help, surrounding your eyes and ears with the pure gospel teaching. Ask Him for help to rid your home of the mixture (favor by works) teaching.

_____

_____

_____

_____

_____

_____

_____

_____

_____

_____

_____

_____

_____

_____

_____

_____

_____

_____

_____

Day 20
Grace Brings Newness

When asking my kids to clean their rooms, now that they are teenagers, I get a little more push back because they know my room is not clean either! You see, I have good intentions of keeping my bedroom clean but it doesn't always happen.

Needless to say, God is a much better parent than I am. He did the cleaning part for us (what we couldn't do) and all He asks of us is to agree by faith. He says we are forgiven, and are not only clean, but have also become new creations in Christ Jesus! We have been adopted as sons and daughters!

His Word says we were crucified with Jesus, and we no longer live, but Christ lives in us. He actually made our spirit one with Him and declares us holy and righteous, expecting us to declare the same. Praise God we have been cleansed and have been given a new heart and new spirit!

— Brandon Pollard

Scripture Meditation:
Ezekiel 36:25-27 (English Standard Version)

I will sprinkle clean water on you, and you shall be clean from all your uncleanness, and from all your idols I will cleanse you. And I will give you a new heart, and a new spirit I will put within you. And I will remove the heart of stone from your flesh and give you a heart of flesh. And I will put my Spirit within you, and cause you to walk in my statutes and be careful to obey my rules.

Grace Challenge:

Ask the Lord if someone you know needs to hear the good news about their new identity. Make a phone call and invite them to church. Offer to pick them up and invite them to lunch afterwards.

_____

_____

_____

_____

_____

_____

_____

_____

_____

_____

_____

_____

_____

_____

_____

_____

_____

_____

_____

Day 21
Grace For Eternity

My heart grieves when hearing people say God in Heaven is judging the earth today with natural catastrophes.

Did the cross do *anything*? Do we, the body of Christ, not understand 2 Corinthians 5:19 that we are called to the ministry of *reconciliation*? To proclaim to all: God's not counting the world's sins against them!

Some teachers perceive the judgment of God is happening now and they believe the church will be removed shortly with even greater punishment released on the earth. Fear takes hold of many Christians and of course, the altars flood with those needing to get re-saved again.

Jesus is not a liar, if someone was able to predict His return, then He would not have said in Matthew 24:36, "But concerning that day and hour no one knows, not even the angels of heaven, nor the Son, but the Father only." (English Standard Version)

When Jesus was on earth, he went to the synagogue, opened the scroll, and chose to stop at Isaiah 61, reading aloud about His own ministry, "to proclaim the year of the Lord's favor." Even if he had continued to quote, "and the day of vengeance of our God", vengeance was against Satan, not people. While there will be a "Day of Judgment", when all will stand before God and give an account of our lives (Matthew 12:36), it is a future set time that only the Father knows. Right now, we are in the year (season) of the Lord's favor!

After Jesus' resurrection, He gave the disciples the same ministry to proclaim the year of the Lord's favor. The Holy Spirit was poured out at Pentecost to many of the very people who denied and crucified Jesus. Can you imagine what the penalty should have been for crucifying the God of the universe? However, instead of judgment, three thousand people were born again!

It is the same today. Every man, woman and child today can receive the same Holy Spirit when they are born again. That is favor from God! So if Jesus made it His ministry on earth to proclaim the Lord's favor, shouldn't we share God's grace for eternity as well?

— Brandon Pollard

Scripture Meditation:

1 John 4:16-19 (English Standard Version)

So we have come to know and to believe the love that God has for us. God is love, and whoever abides in love abides in God, and God abides in him. By this is love perfected with us, so that we may have confidence for the day of judgment, because as he is so also are we in this world. There is no fear in love, but perfect love casts out fear. For fear has to do with punishment, and whoever fears has not been perfected in love. We love because he first loved us.

Grace Challenge:

Share the good news with a stranger or unsaved friend today, that God loves them and is not angry with them. Tell them God provided Jesus as a sacrifice for their sins and ask them if they would like Jesus to save them for eternity.

_____

_____

_____

_____

_____

_____

_____

_____

_____

_____

_____

_____

_____

_____

_____

_____

_____

_____

About the Authors

Brandon and Dana Pollard co-founded Grace For Eternity Church in 2015 with a desire to proclaim the gospel of grace in Fort Worth, TX.

The Grace Team are people who volunteer their time and talents to the Lord at Grace For Eternity Church and have laid their life down for the advancement of the gospel.

Donate Today

By supporting this ministry, you are sowing into the Kingdom of God by allowing us to reach people who never would have otherwise heard that they are valued, worthy and loved by the Father in heaven.

Many put their faith in Christ for the first time through Grace For Eternity and their lives are radically changed.

Many are set free from guilt, condemnation, and fear because they have never heard the gospel of grace; they've only heard religion that sets us up for continual failure.

Thank you for partnering with us!

Mailing Address:

Grace For Eternity Ministries

4360 Western Center Blvd Box 207

Fort Worth, TX 76137

www.graceforeternity.com

Index

Contributors:
Gary Seay
Mark Hamilton
Kim Hamilton
John Phillips
Kati Phillips
Gail Gause

Bible Translations Used:
English Standard Version
New Living Translation
New King James Version
King James Version
New International Version